Viva il Sonetto

Sonnets by Steve Elliott

ISBN: 978-93-6354-550-2

First Edition: 2026
Rs. 200/-

Cyberwit.net
HIG 45 Kaushambi Kunj, Kalindipuram
Allahabad - 211011 (U.P.) India
http://www.cyberwit.net
Tel: +(91) 9415091004
E-mail: info@cyberwit.net

Printed at Repro India Limited.

Shall I compare thee to a summer's day?

Contents

A salute to the sonnet 7
Dedication 12
Lockdown with Umberto 14
1957 15
Rites of Passage 16
Ghost 17
Memory of Trout 18
Dear William 19
Golden Girl 20
Not Scrabble! 21
Bill of Rights 22
Stuff the Apocalypse 23
9/11 24
The Asylum 25
Huxley 26
To the West 27
Cynthia 28
Sonnet #18* 29
Mermaid Hair 30
Red October 31
Swan 33
Four-Minute Mile 34
Climate Change 35
The Fog 36
The Dog's Story 38
Toad 39
Fragments 40
When You're Young 41
Sun-kissed Ages of Childhood 42

1969 43
Opium Eaters 44
In Xanadu 45
Dead Poets 46
Adonais 48
e.e. cummings 49
Julia 51
Aristocrat 52
End of the line 53
Coffee 54
From a Balcony 55
St Basil's 56
Pushkinville 57
Distant as a star 59
The Art of Love 60
Krypton Baby 61
The Tongue 62
Fast-food Blouse 63
Waiting 64
Flower 65
Library Bouquet 66
Last Day, Pompeii 67
Confessio 68
How to write a sonnet 69
Hey Horace! 70
Sonnets and stuff 71

A salute to the sonnet

While some collect matchboxes, others of a more literary bent horde sonnets. The form has been around forever. I personally find it highly addictive. In fact, there may well be a surfeit of sonnets on my shelves. At first glance, stark on the page, a sonnet looks a little forbidding: it's a box, a kind of padded cell containing 14 lines of iambic pentameter, with a prescribed rhyme scheme, if we are talking about Petrarchan (Italian sonnets) and/or Shakespearean sonnets. A sonnet is a stringent workout for the poetic muscles and the mathematics of the form is intriguing. You have just 14 lines to state your case. You must introduce your subject, elaborate upon it, and then change gear in the final part to wrap it up neatly in the last two lines, while obeying (or not, as the case may be) matters of meter and rhyme. You may do as Petrarch did and write an octave (8 lines) and then pivot via a volta into a contrasting final sestet (6 lines). Or you could write three quatrains and finish with a couplet as William Shakespeare favoured. Either way, it's a Houdini act, in which the poet battles with the chains of rhyme and meter in order to release a satisfying poetic conclusion and transcend the confines of the sonnet's box.

In terms of form, anything goes these days. The sonnet has been bashed about from pillar to post by countless soneteers for about 800 years. It is a durable poetic force that has engaged the minds and quills of many great poets, including Spenser, Shakespeare, Milton, Shelley, Keats, Tennyson, Millay, Auden, Larkin... Writers of other languages also exploited the form, starting with the pioneer, the Italian Petrarch; Verlaine and Rimbaud wrote sonnets in French; Rilke's *Sonnets to Orpheus* are a landmark in German literature, while the great Argentinian poet Jose Louis Borges wrote yards of sonnets in Spanish. It is fruitless, of course, to give a full list of history's celebrated soneteers. They are legion. A pantheon.

By the way, you can blame the Italians for sonnets. The name comes from *sonetto*, which in Italian means little song. The form was invented in Italy by a thirteenth-century notary named Giacomo da Lentini. While Giacomo may well have been a fine lawyer, he wasn't such hot stuff as a poet. However, Petrarch, an Italian genius in the Dante mould, perfected and popularised the form in the 14th century. In the 16th century, William Shakespeare took up the reins and gave the sonnet another vigorous head of steam. He invented his own sonnet form: the aforementioned three quatrains and a couplet to finish. Since then, every poet and his dog has written sonnets.

But what makes them tick? What's under the hood of the sonnet's rather sleek and compact body? It goes back to that mechanical talk of pivots and voltas earlier. Usually, a problem or situation is set up, expanded upon, and then by means of a volta (Italian for turn) the poem changes its perspective and/or tone, to resolve the whole idea neatly at the end. We can illustrate this with a Petrarchan scheme employed by the American poet, Edna St. Vincent Millay. The first line is also the title:

What lips my lips have kissed, and where, and why,
I have forgotten, and what arms have lain
Under my head till morning; but the rain
Is full of ghosts tonight, that tap and sigh
Upon the glass and listen for reply,
And in my heart there stirs a quiet pain
For unremembered lads that not again
Will turn to me at midnight with a cry.

Thus in the winter stands the lonely tree,
Nor knows what birds have vanished one by one,
Yet knows its boughs more silent than before:
I cannot say what loves have come and gone,

I only know that summer sang in me
A little while, that in me sings no more.

In the first eight lines (the octave), the poet talks about her apparently ambivalent romantic attachments: 'I have forgotten', 'For unremembered lads.' She can't even recall the names of her lovers but all the same… She is haunted, the night is 'full of ghosts', and the author mourns the transcient nature of love. In the last six lines (the sestet), she uses a classic volta word, 'Thus', to change the perpective and tone entirely. The poem now becomes metaphorical: her love is compared to a withered and lonely tree in a barren winter landscape. Its branches are bare; all the birds have flown. The final realisation is somewhat bleak, a fitting resolution to the sestet's theme of winter's implacable desolation and silence.

To write a decent sonnet is akin to a magic trick. It requires great powers of brevity and the ability to distill, not to mention a potent poetic vision. The poet must conjure something within the strict bonds of 14 lines, and produce the extraordinary rabbit out of the literary hat to delight the reader. A great sonnet has the power of a great novel in the way it resonates in the mind, long after reading, illuminating something that is true and compelling, something that moves the reader and connects with their own experience. In short, the poet can say a whole lot in 14 lines and evoke a number of emotions. Possibly my favourite sonnet in the English language, Shelley's *Ozymandias*, manages to encompass something of truly epic proportions, while, incidentally, breaking Petrarchan and Shakespearian rules. Allow me to be extravagant and quote it in full here:

I met a traveller from an antique land,
Who said—"Two vast and trunkless legs of stone
Stand in the desert. . . . Near them, on the sand,

Half sunk a shattered visage lies, whose frown,
And wrinkled lip, and sneer of cold command,
Tell that its sculptor well those passions read
Which yet survive, stamped on these lifeless things,
The hand that mocked them, and the heart that fed;
And on the pedestal, these words appear:
My name is Ozymandias, King of Kings;
Look on my Works, ye Mighty, and despair!
Nothing beside remains. Round the decay
Of that colossal Wreck, boundless and bare
The lone and level sands stretch far away."

Ozymandias is a poem of immense depth and withering insight. The blunt message is that power corrupts and the monuments you raise to celebrate your dominion will inevitably crash and tumble in time, as the once-mighty Ramses II and his empire crumbled to dust, erased by the 'lone and level sands'. To quote myself from a sonnet in this book, 'Tides turn, Rome fiddles, emperors burn.'

I mentioned that Percy Shelley followed neither Shakespeare's nor the Italian Sonnet's formulae. Poets are of course at liberty to stretch their legs, and their pens. A striking example is *Carrion Comfort* by the 19th century English poet Gerard Manley Hopkins. The poem has lines like these: 'O in turns of tempest, me heaped there; me frantic to avoid thee and flee?' By no means is it iambic pentameter. Hopkins pushed and stretched the boundaries of the sonnet till the pips squeaked, inventing a new way to count meter called sprung rhythm. Thus, have poets tinkered with 14 lines over the centuries.

It should be said that not all people in the poetry game salute the sonnet. The form has some heavyweight detractors. For instance, Byron hated writing them and refered to sonnets as, 'The most puling, petrifying, stupidly platonic compositions.' Ezra Pound denounced the sonnet, calling it 'The Devil!' He maintained it was an outmoded and rigid 'blueprint', an archaic monument that should be abandoned and left in antiquity where it rightly belongs. It was a view shared by many modern poets. W.H. Auden, although he did write some sonnets, called it a 'trap' due to its celebrated history and sheer literary baggage. But I'll go with William Wordsworth who said, 'Scorn not the sonnet.' From Larkin to Lowell, many modern poets have heeded Wordsworth's advice and sonnets continue to be written. As a form, it has endured and will endure, because it has proved to be a robust, shiny, and versatile poetic vehicle. *Viva il sonetto!*

Steve Elliott

Dedication

Now here's a different kind of dedication,
(But I'll omit the folk I met on vacation!)
Obviously that's not crucial. But I digress,
With a panegyric to mustard and cress,
To climbing the crags of a Cornish coast,
And to Mr. Oscar Wilde for his wittiness.
I might've dedicated this to Kerouac's ghost,
But I remember Mum and Dad, especially,
And all the ancestors in the family tree.
Otherwise, this dedication could not be.
I say it, finally, but it's first and foremost;
You save the best till last, of course:
I dedicate this to my muse, my wife,
And to Love which is the best of life.

‘Scorn not the sonnet’

WILLIAM WORDWORTH

Lockdown with Umberto

In lockdown, I read *Foucault's Pendulum.*
Hermetically sealed, far from the clan,
In quarantine, chronicling a saeculum.
It started with Templars in the Holy Land.
The plan was detailed, and hard to follow,
Esoteric, arcane, a mouthful to swallow.
My grasp of the mythologies proved weak,
I twisted and flailed, beached on the sand.
Some ideas seemed as baffling as Greek.
In places, I found I was lost — up the creek!
I encountered the madness of windmills,
I beat about a burning bush, raising dust.
On map-less questing through Judaean hills,
I realised: a classical education is a must.

1957

I'm practically Victorian! Let me explain:
Being born in Nineteen Fifty-Seven,
Five decades had seen Victoria in Heaven.
Today, you may say, 'Isn't it lame
To lay such a claim? Surely, it's a joke?'
But this is what I have always said:
A bunch of Victorians fucked with my head.
It's not really my mum and dad to blame;
They'd had a belly full of hiding the booze
From Victorian stiffs, temperance folk.
Despite Dr. Freud breaking the news,
They rammed purity down their throat:
Strict, forbidding, implacable as a purge
That made you ashamed of the sexual urge.

Rites of Passage

All that razzmatazz and splitting of sides,
Haring off to county fair west of Winchester!
Promise of dizzy blondes and dizzier rides,
Candy floss copped with kisses besides.
Past sheep dips and a combine harvester
Towards the blue hills beyond. Here's a bridge,
A winding river, a brackish pond.

But upwards now, and over the ridge.
Another cattle grid. We slide and skid
Towards bacchanals of beer and song
And distant laughter. Young rascals stand
And deliver; young ladies are all a-quiver:
Sweating, swinging to Rock 'n' Roll bands,
Sex and saxophones swelling the glans.

Ghost

This one has the pallor of a ghost—
These morbid mirrors reflect a self;
It must be an actor, surely not me!
And suddenly swimming into sight,
Slender volumes of Larkin's poetry.
Then flotsam and jetsam, bits of time,
Desires unreachable as a high shelf.
One hot summer on the Dorset coast,
And they sang, *Baby please be mine!*
Yellow sand slipped through my hand.
Fingerprints at the scene of the crime.
The clues mount, and come to light,
But it's beyond what's here and now;
All that is so far removed, somehow.

Memory of Trout

Upside down in a camera obscura,
Asking have I moved on any further,
After the wrench of upping sticks
And coming to a place like this?
The cold panorama, the bleak block,
The paradox of a singular red sock.
I might say, it all began back then…
Far away by a weeping willow tree
Shading seven stepping stones,
Where rainbow trout rose in a river,
Winding passed lobelia and hollyhock.
That was all so long ago, although,
I see them still, darts in the flow —
Electric, elusive, pure quicksilver.

Dear William

Dear William, I don't require a poem
About clouds and daffodils and what not.
I need something with more… backbone.
Look what's happening on the street:
Pandemonium! So *you* must bear the brunt
Of coming up with something crisp and neat,
Something thoroughly, existentially modern.
Really, my dear Will, you're on the spot!
You must rise to the challenge; to be blunt,
I need something original, a path untrodden.
Apply yourself, and all of your literary skills
To things other than clouds and daffodils.
They just won't sell, you silly old nitwit—
Come on Will! Make your words worth it!

Golden Girl

for Arina Semenova

She can hide her hair in heavenly hats,
And weave an intricate web of plaits.
Occasionally, she wears it in a ponytail.
And sometimes, just for fun, in a bun.
I like it best when it's loose and free,
Flying in the wind, whipping like a sail.
She is then the epitome of beauty:
Framing her sunlit, dappled face,
Flaxen, fair, the blondest of thread…
I watch the skittish toss of her head,
And her hair cascading back into place.
Then she pins it all up in a pile of gold
And becomes Aphrodite in the sun—
Serene, proud, a goddess to behold.

Not Scrabble!

After lunch, they went to do battle at Scrabble,
And fumbled towards a linguistic jumble…
Want something more gripping to unravel
Than counting the value of 'apple' or 'crumble'?
Here's an activity for slow Sunday afternoons;
I relish it far more than polishing spoons.
So, when you're ready, cut up a bunch
Of words, and some random phrases
Snipped from magazines and other places.
Stick them together and rearrange them.
See what occurs: *the fully-clothed lunch?*
A jellyfish in furs? Whatever the outcome,
It beats having a rack of nothing but 'U',
And praying the next go will turn up a 'Q'!

Bill of Rights

The past is weighed to judge its lessons.
Progressio in futuras, we dish out the blame,
And some contend that what we did
All those years ago was a crying shame.
Are these peculiarly modern obsessions?
Should we grasp and lift the grimy lid,
Claiming we shouldn't have said this or that
About any old sex, or white or black,
About the dog days and dark nights,
That we should rewrite the Bill of Rights?
You may ask where all this will end.
We used to enjoy freedom of speech.
Is it something you can bend out of reach
Simply by having a big enough spend?

Stuff the Apocalypse

These days I stare through windows
At friendly leaves waving from trees.
I spend hours contemplating motes
Of sunlight percolating on parquet.
I magnify tiny worlds through a lens,
To grasp perhaps a bigger picture,
And some few harmonious notes.
Anything to stall the flights of hysteria,
The *Whitehall Farce* of an idiotic world
Dropping its trousers and shitting bricks.
It isn't real, so stuff your apocalypse!
Let me peel the headlines from my eyelids
And fling them in the garbage,
Or recycle them into wings of doves.

9/11

Some things barely make any sense.
I forget what I ought to remember
And then recall what I should forget.
Today is the 11th of September;
I am reminded of towers falling.
Who knows what really happened
In between brazen lies and regret,
And all the headlines screaming…

Did that mad old sheikh lose his mind
While the world was lost and dreaming?
The president's men came calling,
Killed him like a dog one morning.
Then they all came off the fence,
And there was war, famine, pestilence!

The Asylum

From the asylum, the lines are drawn:
Rules adhered to; protocol observed;
The business of war, which is a given.
They bark out orders, blurting slogans
From a bullhorn in a hall of mirrors.
Times are strange, read between lines.
Mark the cicatrix. The disease is fear;
A digital smear, miasmic as McDonald's.
Truth and Beauty are no longer permitted.
There is only this way or the highway:
A brand-new lifestyle in a straitjacket.
Get ear-plugs to diminish the racket!
THE END will appear on screen,
For whatever eyes are left to see it.

Huxley

Hey robot! You robot! I robot!
Programed to walk under a bus
Should we cause too much fuss.
You, cyberborg with connected arm,
Jabbed with stuff that causes harm!
And all that hysteria over bits of snot.

Pretty soon, you'll be needing an app,
Be programed when to take a crap,
And when and if, you should piss!
Is there no way to stop the rot?
Beast and claw, labeled 666!
Huxley said it would come to this.
Who knows how it'll all turn out?
How long before we all burn out?

To the West

To the West the bridges are broken.
Fissures and cracks scar the land.
There's no going back. They've spoken:
A line has been drawn in the sand.
Democracy isn't what it used to be
And communism's gone right out of fashion.
Half the world struggles to be free
And half dies for a fairer ration.

Thus, the bridge stands there battered,
No way to cross the raging torrent.
Those who stand on the eastern banks
Reject the West and its tiresome warrant.
Razed by bombs, harried by tanks,
They've seen their land ravaged and scattered.

Cynthia

Swift clouds ply peculiar boats above
Her: white sails gliding across the face
Of the moon, full and beaming its love,
Inspiring the unbridled tide to race
Up the shore and hiss over the sand.
She closes it all in the palm of her hand,
A pearl to glisten deep within a pocket.
She cannot speak of Cynthia, long dead,
Held close to heart in a golden locket.
There are many things she leaves unsaid,
But a note is written so they may trace
The dark side cratered inside her head.
She will not be released from this lunacy,
And wades out to sink in a moonlit sea.

Sonnet #18*

Shall I compare *thee* to a London bus,
Or the backend of one? Your hair *is* red!
No! You're quite thin, face tinted green,
So, I compare *thee* to a traffic light instead.
'Specially as amber's your favourite colour.
I saw you flashing on and off in a dream.
What was that on your jumper? An incubus?
Something with legs… Frankly, a horror.
And your moods do change like the lights:
One moment you smile, the next you frown.
And so it goes on and on for days and nights.
When you're on red, I brake and slow down;
But when you go green… How sublime:
It's roses, red wine, and *whooppee* time!

*Apologies to William Shakespeare

Mermaid Hair

The tide has risen,
swamped the beach.

The pretty mermaids
swept out of reach.

The upper air
choked with clouds.

The rain is thinning
out the crowds:

They divide and scamper
across the square,

Silting up the shelter—
bare inches to spare.

While I dream
and drown in mermaid hair.

Red October

October! How the spendthrift trees
Squander their legions of leaves:
Tumbling notes of copper and gold.
Spring and summer's hot routine
Kept the balance crisp and green.
But red October ushers in the cold
And winter rehearses in the wings.
About the house, a shrill wind sings
From skies as miserable as Mondays.
The chill-eyed banker appears on cue,
Demanding what is clearly past due:
A golden raiment strewn at his feet;
More leaves than you could sweep
In a month of gruelling Sundays.

‘A trap’

W.H. AUDEN

Swan

For Galina Samsova

Perfected synthesis of body and mind.
What is she if not poetry in motion?
Sinew and muscle that fluidly find
Precisely the poise, rhythm and flow
Of a choreographed intricate design.
She's lifted high on a crest of emotion
That carries its force beyond the stage,
Rolling over the audience like a wave.
Breathless, we witness the dying fall,
Then the flourish, and the final bow;
Argosies of bouquets are presented now.
She's like her flowers, fragile and small.
Grace and beauty! A rapturous refrain.
But are those tears of happiness, or of pain?

Four-Minute Mile

For Steve Ovett

Lean of limb, milers are a special breed:
Four even quarters 'gainst clock and man;
Rare combo of endurance and speed.
Opponents and the ticking hand:
Four laps under a four-minute span.
The gun propels the mile into its stride,
The pace is brisk and the runners glide.
The first lap unwinds, early in the game,
While the second passes with moderate strain.
Spiked shoes dig into the blood-red track;
The third lap's an exile of mounting pain,
Steeling mind and body for the final attack.
The bell clangs: last quarter to the tape
And the winning kick in the home straight.

Climate Change

1

A lake once lapped a lush green shore
Before an eternity of dust appeared:
Parched, cracked, desolate ground,
Idols slouching in the lost and found.
Eons and eons more. Locusts in hordes.
In the God forge, humanity is cleared.
How much time does time compound?
Ages elapsed before fields of wheat
Rustled again, thriving in rain and heat.
Rise and fall, relapse and collapse!
And how many exiled peoples fled?
Or were put to merciless swords,
Crushed and ground to destruction:
Death knell and final corruption.

2

Another go! We're under starter's orders.
Armageddon's alarming all the same.
Rien ne va plus, bet on the human race,
Embrace all kindness, love and grace.
Wieder, zeitgeist, and some civilised talk,
Winding along the herbaceous borders.
And don't forget to use the right fork!
Mr. Eliot and Dante argue in the pantry.
Folk round here just *come and go...*
While the croupier spins another throw.
Nobody needs a Doctor of Divinity,
Bob Dylan, or even the Holy Trinity
To know which way the Horsemen churn:
Tides turn, Rome fiddles, emperors burn.

The Fog

1

I met Tommy on the pier at Southend:
Days of *Rock against Racism… Dr. Feelgood…*
White Boy on a diet, light as a petal,
Too sharp and too thin for heavy metal.
The frantic jive, the patois, the babble,
Scoring meth from a hood in the back.
In those days, it was the high of fashion.
He called me *Mein Liebling,* his Sistine Chapel.
He mounted my pulpit with all his passion,
Our heads floating not far from the ceiling.
Gabbling on, (you know how it gets),
About Jazz and the holy spirit of Stan Getz:
Myriad connections and crossed wires,
Profanities, vanities, and bonfires.

2

Tonight, he's lit up again, mind streaming;
There is so much, so many things to say,
Insights all gilded with iconic revelation.
Tommy speaks of a visit from Kerouac's ghost,
Then *Pearl & Dean* projected in dreams,
And how to spread butter on hot toast:
Generously, thick, and even, it seems.
Memory slips to his forty-fifth birthday,
When we danced all night with Beaujolais,
Spliffs and poetry, which is Tommy's religion.
Then he loses it: another kick in the psyche!
He insists there is no theological solution,

Although there may be provisional salvation.
Then he rants on about poverty and deprivation.

3

Tommy goes silent and mutters at the wall.
What to do? Well, he does love his trips.
What about taking a southbound train, stall
The gloom, and put a smile on his lips?
Storm the old pier, jukebox switch in hand,
Then leapfrog like lunatics across the sand.
Ah! Wouldn't that be utter blissfulness?
But we're crashing now like the breakers.
Eyes telegraphing a bleary wistfulness,
Tommy begins to fumble for his works,
To drift oblivious on a pillow of poppies.
And over the drear, dilapidated acres,
And the two-up-two-down terraced sprawl,
A fog begins to fall.

The Dog's Story

For the Trelawny-Ross family

This is the dog's side of the story:
'I locked *Mother Hubbard* in the cupboard,
For which I wasn't in the least bit sorry.
I then pranced off to the pantry,
Where I discovered a fantasy,
A feast beyond canine dreams:
A nice juicy leg of lamb;
Bacon hanging in reams;
A barrel of salted pork,
And a whole side of ham.
Gosh, what nosh! I thought.
Let's get stuck in and dine in style.'

So, that poor old *Mother Hubbard*
Languished in the cupboard a while!

Toad

Keats wrote a poem about a Grecian urn,
But he didn't pen an ode about a toad:
Marvellous toady in his loamy abode.
From the toad you have much to learn.
This amphibian is ecologically sound,
Eating pests that can ruin the ground.
See how he lurks in the damp grasses,
Meditating on a slug's slow, silver track,
Over leaves, twigs and stony passes.
Pondering the moment of his final attack,
The toad is an object lesson in patience;
He keeps your garden under surveillance.
Inscrutable as a sphinx, still as a stone,
For what can the marvellous toad atone?

Fragments

These fragments fly in, loud, even
Deafening through summer's open window:
Exclamation, hiss, and rising pitch!
A wife wants a new three-piece suite,
But the husband appears disinclined,
And what's wrong with the old one?
The question mark hangs in limbo,
Answered by the slow creak of shutters
And receding footsteps in the stifling night.
Then, someone argues the price of petrol
Is indivisibly linked to a vicious cabal
Of witches and other *sons of bitches*!
These fragments swirl in a capricious wind
That can never agree the direction it's in.

When You're Young

When you're young, time stretches far ahead—
Wide as an ocean, a gulf from shore to shore.
That it has an end somewhere is unimaginable;
It is practically limitless, and what is more,
All things are possible. Death is intangible.
Time vanishing doesn't fill you with dread.
For a child, the future is distant and dim,
But when you grow old and your hair is thin,
The weeks and months fly at an alarming rate.
You wish you could arrest the blasted clock:
Its hands race and you want to put a brake
On its headlong speed and make it STOP!

When you're young, time is your best friend;
It's like a summer that seems to know no end.

Sun-kissed Ages of Childhood

In those sun-kissed ages of childhood,
You leaf through pages of once upon a time.
You learn through play, and that is good.
Later, the world loses some of its shine,
And your role assumes a mask more tragic
In your diversion from wonder and magic.

In those sun-kissed ages of childhood,
You dance on stages, and feel the blood
Supercharging limbs and legs on springs,
As though God had given you wings.

But, in those sun-kissed ages of childhood,
You also have rages, and have understood
The sun goes down and the moon rises—
Night comes with nightmares and surprises.

1969

In his mind it's Nineteen Sixty-Nine.
The American Dream's run out steam.
Uncle Sam? Hunkered down in 'Nam!
No one can pretend the war will ever end.
It's well past the hour of flower power,
Plainly understood there will be blood.
Too soon to send a man to the moon?
Too late to consume what's on our plate?
Too early to pray for Judgement Day?
Too blind to react to the obvious sign?
At wild Woodstock, the hippies rock;
The high watermark recedes in the dark.

But for him, '69 was a fine old time —
Way back then, when he was ten.

Opium Eaters

Death crowds in with a deathly grin.
John and Perce died far too young.
I'm dying myself; it isn't much fun;
There is no cure for tuberculous mud,
And I'm coughing up a sea of blood.
So I called upon old Sam Coleridge,
Begging to partake of some poppy.
The poet groaned, 'Ain't life a bitch?'
I replied, 'Sam, I shall pay you cash,
For I would fain scratch that itch.'
Said he, 'Don't think me stroppy,
But that bastard Byron dropped in
And collared the last of my stash!'

In Xanadu

Here, such poetry and other drugs
Are consumed in equal measure.
Bubbling over, these brimful jugs
Quench the thirst for illicit pleasure.

He reeled in from a drenching spree,
Brain cranked up, screaming for ink,
And parchment to get it all down,
Before it ran off as water down a sink,
Or like a boat subsiding in the sound.

The tinctured resin of Indian gee
Ignited his fevered imagination.
The midnight oil burned on and on.
Yet still, after that fatal interruption,
It remained an unfinished operation.

Dead Poets

1

T.S. Eliot is a titan, a towering figure.
In poetry, it doesn't get much bigger.
Unless we wheel in William— Dear Bill!
Or fan the flames with Dante Alighieri,
Then perhaps, bung in some Chaucer, too.
You know, seriously go for the quill:
A motley, medieval scrivener crew.
The French boast Corneille and Racine,
Heavyweights of the Parisian literary scene.
And don't forget Rimbaud and Baudelaire,
Lest they dropkick you in the *derrière*,
Et peut-être, arrange for the guillotine!

But T.S., whether in poetry or in prose,
Is huge, like the Colossus of Rhodes.

2

The Russians would have a seizure
If we didn't mention their geezer:
Great Alexander Sergeevich Pushkin,
Who wrote epically of Eugene Onegin,
And died duelling with a bullet in his skin.
And what about Herrs Goethe and Schiller?
The Germans had a few crack scribes.
Later on came Thomas Mann and Hesse;
They didn't always split your sides,

But *Dr. Faustus* was quite a thriller.
Yet, you have to hand it to Thomas Stearns.
He certainly knew his Grecian urns.

Anyway, trusting it won't spark any spats,
I like *Old Possum's Book of Practical Cats*.

Adonais

For David Trelawny-Ross

A lowering sky broods over dark water.
If you dare you die, my dearest Percy!
Look Shelley, it will give you no quarter.
Why throw yourself at the storm's mercy?
Why choke in a watery ring of foam?
Preserve your skin, please stay at home!

But Percy was blind and loosed the rope
That held the boat fast in safe haven.
The poet set sail against all the advice
Of Edward Trelawny and his raven.

He drowned in the bay, passing to history;
They burned his body on a pyre at Lerici.
And Mary S. had a wish that could not be:
'Restore my dearest Percy Bysshe to me!'

e.e. cummings

Slam dunk stanzas and tricky bonanzas
Stashed in the trash with *Ogden Nash*
And the other wags at the *New Yorker*!
Let's have a bardy bash: *James Thurber*
On the witty committee with *Walter Mitty*!
We'll serve soft drinks. Think of the kiddies!

give us break: whisky straight for pete's sake!
with a dash of e.e. cummings to chase.
e.e. eschewed for shocks, extravaganza (?)
capital letters in any position or case
and was rave(ly) reviewed or maybe not
for his punctuation (brackets) comma

Well that's it, Dot! You've had your lot.
I really couldn't stand another stanza!

‘

The Devil!’

EZRA POUND

Julia

Julia is a treasure, a real English rose.
Julia is a pleasure wherever she goes.
Julia can be cruel, so brittle and bright,
But Julia's a jewel dazzling in the light.
Julia glitters in an expensive pose,
She's the measure that keeps men on their toes.
She has a tycoon, at whom she hollers;
He owns a bank, brimming with dollars.

Julia needs renewal in the heat of the night,
And the lady has a rule: she's always right.
Julia is a queen, she will brook no veto;
When Julia comes to call, it's incognito.
For Julia is as crimson as a courtesan:
It's a thousand guineas to kiss her hand!

Aristocrat

The Rt. Hon. Toby Bollock raises a bleary eye.
His rooms in Eaton Square elicit a weary sigh:
The antique tables bleed narcotic odours —
Bricks of hash, pills, poppers and powders.
Clouds bloom impressively from Lord J's mouth.
Mandy Q, high class bint, cracks a bottle of fizz.
Lord J remarks that his brains have gone south,
And regards the *ingénues* nose-down in the whizz.

Toby rises and farts, he's desperate for a piss.
Lady Jane reclines on velvet cushions, the drug
Is a blunderbuss, a bumper-car ass…
Couples disport live porno on a Persian rug.
Toby totters towards the writhing mass,
Unzips his gigantic and slashes like a hydrant.

End of the line

Why is the voice at the end of the line
Often resisted with emotions of dread?
The answer's natural human reluctance:
Pushy sales folk hawking internet,
Or some psycho invading your head;
Importunate voices trying to interest you
In your death and who will pay for it;
The bank on your back about your balance;
Your ex-wife screaming for redress;
Pain recriminating in a ghastly whine:
Blaming, shaming… such bitterness!
I'm so sorry! It's a bad connection…
Then static, and the line goes dead,
Leaving a dial tone of accusation.

Coffee

At the blue border of morning,
The birds repeated chorus chirps.
I turn towards the filtered light
And listen to the street that jars
The quiet with commuting cars.
Another day, another dawning!
I give thanks that nothing hurts
And didn't die in that awful flood,
In nightmares of fright and flight.
The day has swallowed up the stars,
The sun has elbowed out the moon.
Shaking, I put down my coffee cup
And reach out for the sugar spoon.
Soon, I shall have woken up.

From a Balcony

On the second-floor balcony, a bloke is smoking.
Higher up, shaded faces stare out at the city's
Spread glare, blinding in the morning sunshine.
Below, the sidewalk actors are: an old man
Shuffling along the expanse of unforgiving tarmac;
His wife stays five patient paces in front of him,
Gazing back through the decades at a younger man.
Along from the left two schoolboys are hurrying,
Followed by a beautiful girl, high heels clacking.
And from the right comes a lady pushing a pram.
A yellow taxi idles along, held up by a delivery van.
The playground opposite whoops and hollers:
Ecstatic children go simian on the apparatus.
Then, a young man flashes by, on a scooter.

St Basil's

Cathedral of Intercession of the Virgin by the Moat!
A bit more of a mouthful than St. Basil's, to be fair. Some say it
resembles a confectioner's fantasy boat. Barefoot supplicant,
Basil the Blessed walked there,
His wonders to perform. The temple's history began
Sometime before its keystone was laid,
With blood, storm, and drums of war in Tatarstan, And Ivan's
dread promise before he smote Kazan:

Bring the Tartar to heel, let him taste Our Russian steel.
Or trample the cur, slice him with a Muscovy blade!
When he kneels, broken before Us, in supplication,
We shall build a cathedral to commemorate the occasion.

Those scenes inhabit a history thankfully remote,
While today, St. Basil's remains cheerfully afloat.

Pushkinville

The bells rang out in Petersburg's cathedrals.
Thin yellow tapers flickered before the icons.
Worshippers nodded and crossed themselves,
Stepping forward to plant supplicant kisses
On some saint's head or the Mother of God.

Out on Nevsky Prospekt, a Russian heroine
Stepped out proudly in high scarlet boots.
Tall, svelte and raven-haired she was.

Later, a light supper at the Literary Cafe.
Alexander Pushkin ate his last meal there.
Then, pistols at dawn by the Black River,
Where the mist rolled in like a shroud,
Sealing his mantle of greatness forever.

‘The most puling, petrifying, stupidly platonic compositions.’

BYRON

Distant as a star

My lady, I worship you from afar,
But I am light years from your station.
Indeed, you are as distant as a star
Shining in some far constellation.
I cannot swim across an ocean;
A fathomless gulf lies between us.
May as well ask for the hand of Venus!
Of course, it is a ridiculous notion.
And so, you must remain a starry icon,
At once the object of lust and devotion.
There is no logic that sheds light on
The cause of impossible infatuation.

My lady, I worship you from afar.
Indeed, you are as distant as a star.

The Art of Love

How *do* you describe the art of love?
How *do* you do it justice enough?
Is it as wanton as wild flowers
Dripping after summer showers?
As deep as a dream can wet?
As wide as a stream can get?

Love's as warm as the aureate light
That is filling you now with desire:
Those languorous limbs that lie
Curled around your lover's thigh!
The art of love requires soft fire
And whispers of amorous intent;
An art as smooth as velvet night,
As sweet as a woman's scent.

Krypton Baby

You're my Krypton Baby,
You superhero you!
You slay me, slay me!
The shuddering crescendo plays me.
Supine I lie with insipid eyes,
Stroking the gossamer hair
On the rill of your thighs.

You're my Krypton Baby,
You slay me, slay me!
I am silly putty in your hands.
I'd write you a sonnet if I could,
But the ink's run dry in my pen.
I may fill it up again,
But there's no telling when.

The Tongue

On the tongue is the language of love
And the language of hate and the language of hunger.
The tongue makes speech possible.
The tongue comforts other tongues that thirst.
But no tongue can restrain a lie unleashed
When that tongue whips up a wave of hate.
The tongue is glib and tells outrageous tales.
The tongue is always a willing instrument.

Juice oozes from those sticky fruits.
Smear your lips with honey, my love,
And kiss me with a game tongue.
Ah, the tongue, the tongue, the tongue!
How many worlds has it undone?
All the power of love is in the tongue.

Fast-food Blouse

'Poets rock!' said the comely waitress.
'Did you see them ones in the Venue?'
Coyly, she prodded my copy of Shelley
With the chewed end of a *Bic* biro
Attached by string to her gingham dress.
I began by squinting over the menu,
And came to rest at ice cream and jelly.
Then I noticed her name was Rita
By the crimson badge on her breast.
Rush of blood, in full view! Gone pyro!
I might have been a tad discreeter,
But I implored that I might kiss her,
For the heaving of that fast-food blouse
Of Rita had not left me unaroused.

Waiting

Are you waiting for something to happen:
Love to bloom like lilies in your room,
A swoon of kisses stolen from the groom,
Or maybe a haiku penned in Japan?

Are you waiting for something to happen:
Someone to hand you riches on a plate,
Someone to say, *You're looking great!*
Or are you hoping the pace will slacken?

Are you waiting for something to happen:
A letter to arrive in the morning post,
An invitation to spend Sunday at the coast?
Something at least, anything to happen:
Weird scenes lit by a magic lantern,
While you wait for something to happen.

Flower

This flower varies in shade, as the rose,
And like the orchid she thrives in heat.
Secretive, her petals are usually closed
But when opened her delights are sweet.
Wreathed in her own special bouquet,
Her crimson lips ooze beads of passion
In arrangements of lubricious display.
This flower is central to God's creation;
For sheer joy she multiplies and blossoms
In the perennial processes of birth.
She embraces the desire of monsoons
To shake her petals and move her earth.
Her nectar flows where the worm slips,
Converting it to succour for human lips.

Library Bouquet

The faintly musty smell of an old book
That has languished on a shelf for ages
Is something I find quite addictive:
Those relict tomes with yellowed pages,
Cut parchment and blocks of wordage.
I spy a thin volume and take a look,
Admiring its rich red vellum spine.
The title is promising, so I open it up.
Couplets swim and drown in the eye;
Shelley's verse verges on the sublime.
I read a poem before closing it shut.

The library bouquet is the reason why
I come here from time to time.

Last Day, Pompeii

Infirm and crabby, Walter Scott's in Rome.
He's come on a mission, far from home,
Itching to see what all the fuss is about,
What English newspapers have been full of—
This new painting by the Russian, Brullov:
Prodigious canvas galvanising sensation;
For painting Vesuvius' legendary eruption,
Brullov is now lionised all over the nation.
It's a masterpiece, stupendous in power:
Pyroclastic cloud spilling choking death,
Scorching Pompeii in its searing breath.
Scott glowers at it for hour upon hour.
Then, finally, utters, *Last Day Pompeii…*
No mere painting, it's a poem, I say!

Confessio

Pardons sought at altars of indulgence,
Like ladies' knickers, gin and bitters,
Pineapple fritters, and what have you not!
Aureate glitter in a blinding effulgence!
This is where they go to stop the rot.
Enter the 3-in-1 identity: the Trinity
And the priests put them on the spot.
For every sort of wrong there's a price;
The measure is stringent and precise:
Your sins are weighed in the balance.
Calibrated by the clicking of the rosary,
You award yourself another chance.
If you simply confess your shame,
You may sin again and again and again.

How to write a sonnet

How do you do it? What's the trick?
Do you glue it? Does it have a wick?
Perhaps if I suffered for this art,
I'd learn to utter a poetic remark:
Starve in an attic, grinding bones,
Deciphering static on headphones.
To crack the rhyme, plumb the depth,
Suck up slime, hold your breath!
Don't be daft! It's all online;
Learn the craft in next to no time:
She wore a bonnet, and sat on a hood,
Cool as a comet, she's looking good.

So, to write a sonnet, start somewhere,
And then get on it! Sound fair?

Hey Horace!

Straight roads and solid foundations…
The Romans were also pavers of poetry.
Famous for being ruthlessly meticulous,
They measured out a metrical scheme.
Compared to the classically sublime,
His efforts are vain, perhaps ridiculous;
Pretender to the art of poetic oratory,
He knocks out a few cheap imitations.
However anxious he may be to climb,
The peak remains a Herculean aim,
A Mount Olympus, a distant dream.
Crashing, burning, losing the game,
He thrashes and turns out second rate
In the shade of what is truly great.

Sonnets and stuff

Another sonnet under the bonnet
And an elegy or two in the boot!
However much you dwell upon it,
That's handsome literary loot.

But when you try to sell the stuff,
The bolts all come unloose:
The carburettor's full of dust;
The spark plugs prove obtuse;
Back-end's hacking black rust,
Exhaust is well and truly bust!

Well, for all the good it's worth,
You could write another quatrain.
You may as well face the truth:
You've got sonnets on the brain.

www.ingramcontent.com/pod-product-compliance
Ingram Content Group UK Ltd.
Pitfield, Milton Keynes, MK11 3LW, UK
UKHW041316190726
13845UKWH00025B/304

9 789363 545502